seeing *with* heart

to journey from within

Alice —

follow your heart, always!

love,

Mitch

seeing *with* heart

to journey from within

The Original Channeled Writings

Dr. Mitch Tishler

LoveYourLife

Love Your Life

Love Your Life Publishing
Wilmington, DE
www.loveyourlifepublishing.com

ISBN: 978-1-934509-89-0
Library of Congress Control Number: 2015955707

Printed in the United States of America
First Printing
Cover design by Ignacio Martinez, www.imcbydesign.com
Seeing With Heart logo by Ray Kingston, www.microspective.net
Back cover photo by Brielle Tishler, www.brielletishlerphotography.com
Editing by Gwen Hoffnagle, www.gwenhoffnagle.com

for you

Contents

Introduction

In 2000, while recuperating from extensive knee surgery, I experienced a compelling feeling to get a blank piece of paper and take a pen in my non-dominant hand. Words flowed and poetic writings revealed themselves. There was no intent to write a book. No conscious awareness of a message. It wasn't until I returned to seeing patients, eighteen months after surgery, that I realized how these writings would support transformational shift. What began happening was fascinating. During an appointment, a patient would share something troubling and I would realize there was a piece in the collection that would support their concern. Regardless the question, there was always a piece that was directly helpful. Over time patients began reporting positive shifts in their daily lives and that they felt the potent medicine contained in these writings. This is how Seeing With Heart™ began.

These writings stand alone and can be used for daily affirmations. Also, you may feel to take the Seeing With Heart journey by reading *Me, Finally*, through a one-to-one experience or attending a retreat. For additional information visit www.seeingwithheart.com.

Embrace the Possibility

THE FOLLOWING WORDS

WALK STRAIGHT INTO THE MYSTERY

FROM WITHIN

the following words

The following words flow as feelings, not thoughts, from the quiet place – the place where all is one. These words are not "mine," yet they have the illusion of flowing through me. Instead, they are core truths that resonate from within each of us. If I felt they were mine, the possibility for receiving them would be not.

To fully know these truths, we must step aside and authentically embrace the possibility of non-ownership. Only in this way are we open to all there is, which is only love, and only then will love flow over all in a way that one only dreams possible.

Now is the time to embrace the possibility – the possibility of Seeing With Heart.

walk straight into the mystery

Walk straight into the mystery in all of its majesty
and fully embrace that which frightens you the most.

Surrender. Let go.

Disregard the expectations of others
(the voices that attempt to bleed your soul)
by offering an unbounded outwardly flowing stream
of unconditional loving kindness.

In your heart, know that the universe always shows up perfectly,
reminding you that some of your most important nourishment
will come from that which tastes awful.

Openly embrace change, as it is not only inevitable – it is life,
providing us the opportunity to see beyond
the limited abilities of our ordinary eyes;
to see that for our spirits to be at peace, they must be at home.

Letting go is the way home, the way back into the stillness.
The place where the miracle is the ordinary not the exceptional.

The place of bliss.

from within

From within
the place of
without expectation,
the universe manifests
expanding peace and harmony,
always and in all ways.

SESSION TWO
Paradigmatic Shift

Through the Illusion

From Afar

There Is a Place

through the illusion

Through the illusion
of physical experience,

Soul speaks directly
to the splintered
piece of peace.

from afar

From afar,
a child calls,
from behind the breeze and before the waves.
Listen, for it is truth.

there is a place

There is a place within each soul
from which the passion stirs the calling,
where the fire drips its luminescence,
birthing the dream place,
the sacred space in time
from which the passion comes to be.

To Journey from Within

SIMPLY BE PRESENT

EMBRACE THE POSSIBILITY

SO OFTEN WE HIDE

SHHH, I HEAR A KNOCKING

IT'S NOT ABOUT THE OUTSIDE

IT IS THE YEARNING

REMEMBER WHEN

simply be present

Simply be present
in the infinite moment,
seeing with heart
not listening with head.

The illusion of faces
the texture of many,
lie not from within
but out at the edge.

Listening with head
will herald the fear,
while seeing with heart
embraces the truth.

There are no many,
there is no separation,
there is only the face of the one.

The face of the present
in the infinite moment,
the face of the truth
in the infinite love.

embrace the possibility

Embrace the possibility
of not thinking about
anything,

expanding instead,

from within the place
of feeling about
everything.

so often we hide

So often we hide
behind "smile at the surface."

Only fooling ourselves,
through the fooling of others.

Rather, smiling from gut
calls the true smile of heart,
flowing out through the eyes,
the true smile of peace.

shhh, i hear a knocking

Shhh, I hear a knocking
from a distant place behind my heart.

Listen – a knocking.
Welcome, come in, I offer with outstretched arms.

As I open my heart I sense
the ethereal movement of joy
welling up as tears of love.

Initially, only vaguely familiar
(from that very distant place).

Then, with imperceptible movement
becoming more present until
finally, uncontainably, flowing over
and passionately caressing
the place where light becomes form.

What, I ask, is this knocking?

Oh, it is me.

it's not about the outside

It's not about the outside,
or even reaching to the in,
for to taste the peace of love,
sip the seeing from within.

it is the yearning

It is the yearning that often drives us
further away from that from which we came.

We look outward
that's what the yearning does.

There must be something, someone, somebody,
any body, any thing, out there to fill the yearning,

kNOw,

it can only be filled by returning to self
by returning to the love from which we came.

remember when

Remember when time had spaces,
remember those sacred drifting places.

Remember to wander,
remember to wonder,
for often the light grows dim.

So let us always remember
our child is calling,
let us all ways listen
from within,
shhh.

SESSION FOUR
Flow from Within

FROM DEEP WITHIN THE MYSTERY

ILLUSION OF EXPANDING OUTWARD

EYES THAT TASTE THE TEXTURE

from deep within the mystery

From deep within the mystery,
somewhere just behind the place of separation,
the illumination of pure love pours out through the heart.

It is here, in this place where the unmanifest begins its journey to form,
that pure love shifts to desire.

This shift is the very foundation of the illusion of separation,
for as desire is drawn out from the heart it slowly infuses the senses
triggering the alluring call from the mind.

The call to the over-wanting and over-needing.

Resist this call with balanced intention, and embrace desire as pure love
by making strong the love of self.

Moving back to the somewhere just behind the place of separation,
where the love of heart leads us from within,
intimately connecting us to all
as one.

illusion of expanding outward

With the illusion of expanding outward,
a spark of pure light begins its journey home.

Along the way, encountering obstacles,
making choices and facing change.

Behind this noise the passionate voice
sings out with steadfast clarity.

A beacon in the fog.

The melody, sacred and singular, is unique only to itself.

Tugging at our core and calling for us to expand from within.

Sing out your melody in all of its majesty,
be your light in all of its purity,
and then you will be home.

So that when the infinity of sparks sings out in collective a capella,
unconditional love will shower bliss on all,
and all will be one.

eyes that taste the texture

With eyes that taste the texture,
look beyond the ordinary.

Expand from within the oneness,
from within the streaming fluid energy
flowing out from and in through
the illusion of the me and the you.

Walk straight into this seeing,
fully tasting this texture,
the texture of the tapestry of one.

SESSION FIVE
Illusion of Separation

Tell Me Everything

An Eyelash

Illusion of Per Chance

tell me everything

"Tell me everything,"
uttered the small child.

"Alright." (pause)
"There is only love.
That is everything,"
whispered the breeze.

an eyelash

An eyelash
resting just a moment above the horizon,
flings out its glitter upon the blackness.

As this fairy dust dances,
the enchanted ocean comes alive,
radiant with luminescent iridescence.

All the while,
the crescent moonrise tugs
at our very cores,
with its invisible strings,
moving our naked souls
as magic marionettes.

Ah, the majesty of miracle.

illusion of per chance

With the illusion of per chance,
our paths crossed,
yet the inner feeling of already knowing
illuminates the thread that connects our souls.

SESSION SIX
Love of Self

EACH MORNING

EVERYTHING BEGINS WITH

AT THE VERY BOTTOM OF MY THROAT

ALONG THE WAY

THE GREAT OPPORTUNITY

HIDING BEHIND MY FAULT

WHY DO WE FIND OURSELVES

each morning

Each morning,
upon rising,
I stretch my arms into the place of truly awakening.

I hug my heart.

everything begins with

Everything begins with loving the self,
yet we're so terribly afraid of "I love me."

We listen instead to the voice that's so haunting,
the one from so far away.

"Don't be so selfish, you must think of the others,
and don't hug yourself or spend time with your soul.
For remember there's nothing to show from these pleasures,
nothing productive, nothing to weigh."

"No!" cries your spirit.

"This is not about selfish, it's about the importance of caring for self.
And doing exactly what one needs in the moment,
by feeling with gut,
the feeling of true."

For being authentic with spirit and soul
is the one single choice that will move us to whole.

Only then can "I love me" and can "I love you"
as they're actually but one in the same.

at the very bottom of my throat

At the very bottom of my throat. That's where.

Oh, you feel it now too. Good, that's the first step.

Go ahead, give yourself permission to embrace this place.

I know, it's bitter, really bitter. And sour, even rancid. Bubbling,
yet not moving. It's so stuck.

Finally, you feel the pain. For so long it wasn't allowed to be any part
of you. Huge denial. That's where all of this stuffed stuff hides,
at the very bottom of our throats wrapped so neatly
in the protective satin lining (of denial).

Go ahead, let it go; groan – let it move.
Yes, it burns (on its way out) – it must.

Let the tears flow; the weeping will dilute the burning,
the caustic burning.

Have trust; in time this burning will pass,
for it is only a surface pain.

The deep pain is the "no pain" of the stuffed stuff.
It is the pain that silently kills us all as we live.

Let us seize the opportunity in this moment of awareness.

Let us let go from that very deep place.

along the way

Along the way, so very many lose their voice.
Later along the way, some few reclaim it.

While, all the while,
even fewer retain that facet
of physical energy
that brings form to the nonphysical sacred contract.

The agreement of soul with the universe.

The very essence behind each individual incarnation.

It is the energy of the "no two identical snowflakes,"
the energy of the "no two identical any things."

It is of that which we are meant to be.

Our truth.

Singular, yet infinite, sacred and sublime.

It is our voice, the authentic voice of soul.

the great opportunity

The great opportunity lies in creating the intention,
and thereby setting the energy in motion,
for retaining – rather than reclaiming – voice.

This is the possibility that we may pass along
to those energies that pass through us – our children,
so that they may flow early and clearly from within the Sacred Contract.

For they are the place of retaining
rather than reclaiming.

hiding behind my fault

Hiding behind "my fault"
is nothing more than running from self.

For remember,
it's our choice to stop (this running),
so that we may shake free
from swirling in the playground of fear,
the dramas that rattle around ever so slightly
below the
surface.

Going beneath this place
will leave "my fault" behind,
breathing movement into the only possibility for true love;
the love of self.

Then, finally,
there is no more running,
from.

why do we find ourselves

But why do we find ourselves
in unwanted places?

Those situations we prefer
to not really be in.

It's all about boundaries and caring for self,
in the love that transcends the illusion of me.

These patterns of being
speak directly to core;
the core of our soul that screams out to be,
in all of its splendor and all of its beauty,
in the fullness of love,
with the all of the we.

SESSION SEVEN
Intimate Connection

INTIMATE RELATIONSHIPS

YET ANOTHER DEAD END

ONE HALF PLUS ONE HALF

BUT WHY DO YOU JUDGE ME

WHEN ALL OF THOSE ABOUT YOU

intimate relationships

It's in our intimate relationships,
those spirit connections
whose threads stretch deeply
from within the sacred,
that we find the possibility
for our greatest healing.

Our choice is to embrace that place,
or not.

yet another dead end

Sadly, I am yet another dead end for you, although the possibility existed that our collective light would ignite the flame of happiness your soul cries out to behold.

You say you want to go there (and then you project your fear, by saying it would be nice if I would be willing to do the same – I am), yet your actions clearly speak a different story.

Larger than life, your dramas become caricatures.
Then you look inward, and your demons pry at your very core, tumbling your soul as a raging wave.

Go ahead; stretch, move through it, not around it.
Go deeper and get to the other side. But no, your head is thinking and you are listening, and so the possibility is broken.

With your frightened eyes, you say it is too big, so you look outward instead, going around, not through. Simply band-aids covering the wound.

Distraction with the illusion of happiness until the rush of adrenalin passes. Desperately, your soul cries out; go in through the heart, go deep through the pain, leave your head and don't turn away.

Keep going until you find the stillness in the quiet place.

The place where happiness is, always.

one half plus one half

One half plus one half
does not equal one,
yet one plus one equals three.

Let us each move closer and closer
to whole and let this simple truth be.

but why do you judge me

But why do you judge me?
Does your heart not feel my compassion?

What blinds your soul from seeing my kindness?
OUCH! Your words, they bite so hard, invisibly bruising.
Why do you hit me in this way?

I know why. You're stuck – stuck big in the fear!

Go ahead or not, it's up to you, go behind this fear,
place your attention on how things are really going in your own life
rather than preoccupying your attention with how you imagine
things are going in mine.

It's not up to me to feel the harmony in your heart, it's up to you.

So free yourself, let go of the fear
and see the sea of peace that lives within your soul,
breathing loving intention into this possibility.

Go ahead, or not!

when all of those about you

When all of those about you
blame all of it on you,
doubt not of yourself but listen instead,
to the voice of the one voice,
as it is your voice, with all of its message so clear.

Tire not of the waiting,
breathe deep into patience,
let go of reaction
and embrace the response.

Only then those who blame you
will listen as well,
to the voice of the one voice,
as it is theirs just the same.

So let's embrace the compassion,
through the possibility of patience,
by pausing to breathe
in the loving response.

Be Present

PEACE AND LIGHT

THE BITTER SCREAMING GALE

LET US RELISH THE CYCLE

SO WHAT DID I DO

peace and light

May peace and light be your chariot,
as that which needs to be, is,
always.

the bitter screaming gale

From within the bitter screaming gale
the soft tranquil smile tenderly embraces
the cold biting wind
while the warm peaceful heart
gently wraps its loving arms
around all who taste the sweetness
in this bitter screaming gale.

let us relish the cycle

Let us relish the cycle,
the cycle of the breathing,
the conduit that is both
the weaver and the weaving.

So effortlessly drawing intention
into each facet of this glittering jewel,
the breathing reminds us that
as we wander along the path,
our work
is to play.

For as we move within its current
we are called to rest often in its eddies,
to imperceptibly inhale the intoxicating illuminations,
caress the undulating tendrils of the iridescent moon rays
and savor, ever so slowly, the succulent dewdrops of dawn.

And so, let us relish both
the weaver and the weaving,
in this eternal rhythmic cycle
of the breathing.

so what did i do

So what did I do through this time called today?

Embrace in the sacred and sip in the moment,
while playing with shadows as they dance with the earth?

Touch the deep mystery by watching a squirrel, a finch, and
a heron, an egret, a rose? A tulip, an orchid, so yellow and crimson
and lavender and scarlet and orange and blue,
and fortunately I forgot not to take in the dew.

The moonrise, the sunset, the song of the breeze,
the sweet wash of nectar so anxious to please.

But oh, now I ponder as my day draws to close,
did I tenderly touch all these morsels of magic?
Or did I just push through my day as a struggle,
a battle to win, just a foe for the conquer –
rushing and blinding the splendor of moment
and stumbling along with my eyes so wide shut?

SESSION NINE
Situation Spiral

SITUATION SPIRAL

SITUATIONS AND DRAMAS

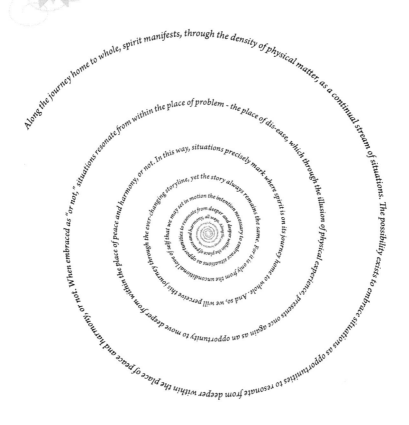

situation spiral

Along the journey home to whole, spirit manifests, through the density of physical matter, as a continual stream of situations. The possibility exists to embrace situations as opportunities to resonate from deeper within the place of peace and harmony, or not. When embraced as "or not," situations resonate from within the place of problem - the place of dis-ease, which through the illusion of physical experience, presents once again as an opportunity to move deeper from within the place of peace and harmony, or not. In this way, situations precisely mark where spirit is on its journey home to whole. And so, we will perceive this journey through the ever-changing storyline, yet the story always remains the same. For it is only from self that we may set in motion the intention necessary to continue resonating situations as opportunities to resonate from deeper and deeper within the place of peace and harmony, all ways, home to the unconditional love of whole.

101

Along the journey home to whole, spirit manifests, through the
density of physical matter, as a continual stream of situations.
The possibility exists to embrace situations as opportunities to
resonate from deeper within the place of peace and harmony, or
not. When embraced as "or not," situations resonate from within
the place of problem – the place of dis-ease, which through
the illusion of physical experience, presents once again as an
opportunity to move deeper from within the place of peace and
harmony, or not. In this way, situations precisely mark where
spirit is on its journey home to whole. And so, we will perceive this
journey through the ever-changing storyline, yet the story always
remains the same. For it is only from the unconditional love of
self that we may set in motion the intention necessary to embrace
situations as opportunities to resonate from deeper and deeper
within the place of peace and harmony, all ways.

situations and dramas

Situations and dramas,
those moments in life
that are often considered problem and conflict
(at times even catastrophe)
are actually the voice of our nonphysical energy
calling out through the illusion
of physical experience.

These moments show up proportionate to
and frequently larger than
the piece of splintered soul.

SESSION TEN
Situation Sphere

SITUATION SPHERE

THE STORYLINE

BEHIND THE FEAR

THE PLACE OF COMPASSION

situation sphere

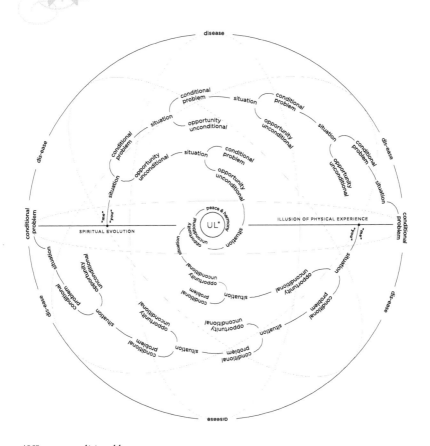

*UL = unconditional love

the storyline

The storyline manifesting in front of source,
(the "me" and the "you")
precisely reflects the proportional balance
of conditional and unconditional energy
as it flows through source.

And while the storyline is always changing,
(through the illusion of human experience)
the story always remains the same.

As we stretch deeper and deeper
from within the authentic unconditional love of self,
the storyline manifests an expanding piece of peace.

behind the fear

Behind the fear
hides abundant unconditional love.

In the fear
resides only conditional love
burdened with expectation.

the place of compassion

From within the place
of compassion, kindness and unconditional love,
the Universe always,
and in all ways,
shows up in abundance.

SESSION ELEVEN
Stillness

One Hand Clapping

Dancing in Stillness

Slowly Sipping Sunshine

In the Stillness

Reaching the Surface

one hand clapping

Like the sound of one hand clapping,
touch the place of no things nothing,
for in this place are all hands clapping,
the silent song of one sound tapping.

dancing in stillness

Dancing in stillness in the nectar of bliss,
the hummingbird motionlessly courts the orchid,
fully embracing the intimacy of interdependence.

Nothing escapes this sharing – this connection – of nourishment
and fertility; nectar and seed.

And so the hummingbird and orchid
passionately stir our souls,
ever-so-brightly illuminating the path.

The path calling us to the dancing in stillness in the nectar of bliss.

slowly sipping sunshine

Slowly sipping sunshine,
drinking stillness from the soul,
the sacred spirit sings out in silent song.

in the stillness

In the stillness of the moment
hides the infinity of the joy.

reaching the surface

Reaching the surface,
the bubble breaks the silence,
which, until that moment,
was like glass in its stillness.

Soft ripples move outward
bringing form to the expanding ethereal energy.

From deep within, another bubble begins to journey upward,
rising as if weightless.

Soon, it too interrupts the surface and the ripples respond by
resonating in harmony.

Over time, the individual bubbles lose their identity,
rising now as one open channel and the ripples dance with glee.

Authentic Power

EMPOWER THE DRAMA

GENTLY STEP BEHIND

STEP OUT FROM THE BOX

OH WHISPERING WIND

empower the drama

Empower the drama
and the power leaks free
from the compassion with boundaries;
the compassion with "me."

Show up instead
with the authentic power
of without expectation;
the true power of "we."

gently step behind

Shhh,
gently step
behind the noise,
softly listening from
within the stillness,
finding "Soul mate"
gently hides within
the sacred peace
called "You."

step out from the box

Step out from the box,
as it's steeped so in fear,
and embrace the flow
of expanding from within;
know that there's nowhere
to go to get there,
for you're already home;
when you're happy, you're "you."

oh whispering wind

Oh whispering wind,
Oh song from the heart.
Beckoning us to dance free from the fear,
by gently embracing our soul as a soft warm blanket.

Providing peace in knowing that we are always home,
no matter how distant we seem to be.

Quietly listen and feel the whispering wind singing out,
as the sensation seeps upward from deep within,
flowing through to the surface;
ever so gently nudging our heart to the awareness of its presence,
like a soft rolling wave caressing the shoreline.

Oh whispering wind.

About the Author

Mitch Tishler, D.C., has presented Seeing With Heart™ – a paradigm-shifting program for cultivating inner peace – to individuals and groups internationally since 2000. Mitch holds a Bachelor of Science Degree with an emphasis in genetics from Connecticut College. He earned his Doctor of Chiropractic Degree from National University of Health Sciences in Chicago, Illinois. Before opening his Wellness Center in Chatham, Massachusetts, in 1987, Mitch backpacked with his former wife through North America, New Zealand, Australia, Asia, and Europe for twelve months, often staying in remote villages and providing healthcare services along the way. In 1988 Mitch co-founded Cape CARES, an international medical relief organization that continues, to this day, to provide critical healthcare services to individuals in the mountains of Southern Honduras. When his children were five and seven years old, the family tent-camped for four months through New Zealand and Australia, and then lived with a Balinese family for two months in Bali, Indonesia. An avid sailor, photographer, musician, and cyclist, you'll find Mitch embracing life along the shores of Cape Cod or at times following his deepest passion, touching people's lives while traveling the world.

Mitch invites you to visit www.mefinally.com and www.seeingwithheart.com for more information.

Made in the USA
Charleston, SC
23 October 2016